through
time
waves

through
time
waves

Marcia Arrieta

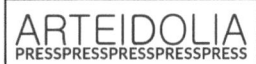

New York

through time waves
Copyright ©2022 Marcia Arrieta. All Rights Reserved.

Special thanks to the editors of Otoliths, Clockwise Cat, After the Pause The South Dakota Review, & Big Scream, where some of these pieces have previously appeared.

Book design: Arteidolia Press
Cover collage: Marcia Arrieta

ARTEIDOLIA PRESS
P.O. Box 157
New York, N.Y. 10276

arteidolia.com/arteidolia-press

First Edition
Library of Congress Control Number: 2022904157
ISBN:978-1-7369983-3-5

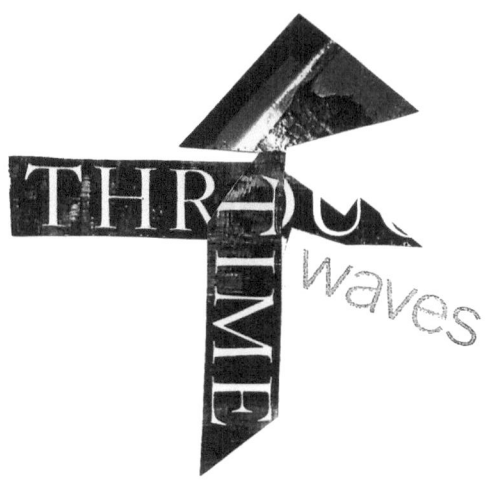

No one realized that the book and the labyrinth were one and the same..
  - Jorge Luis Borges

*to travel in the incandescent we leave the world—
we travel though clouds*
  - H.D.

Not form, but forming—not form as an ultimate phenomenon, but form in the process of being formed as creation.
  - Paul Klee

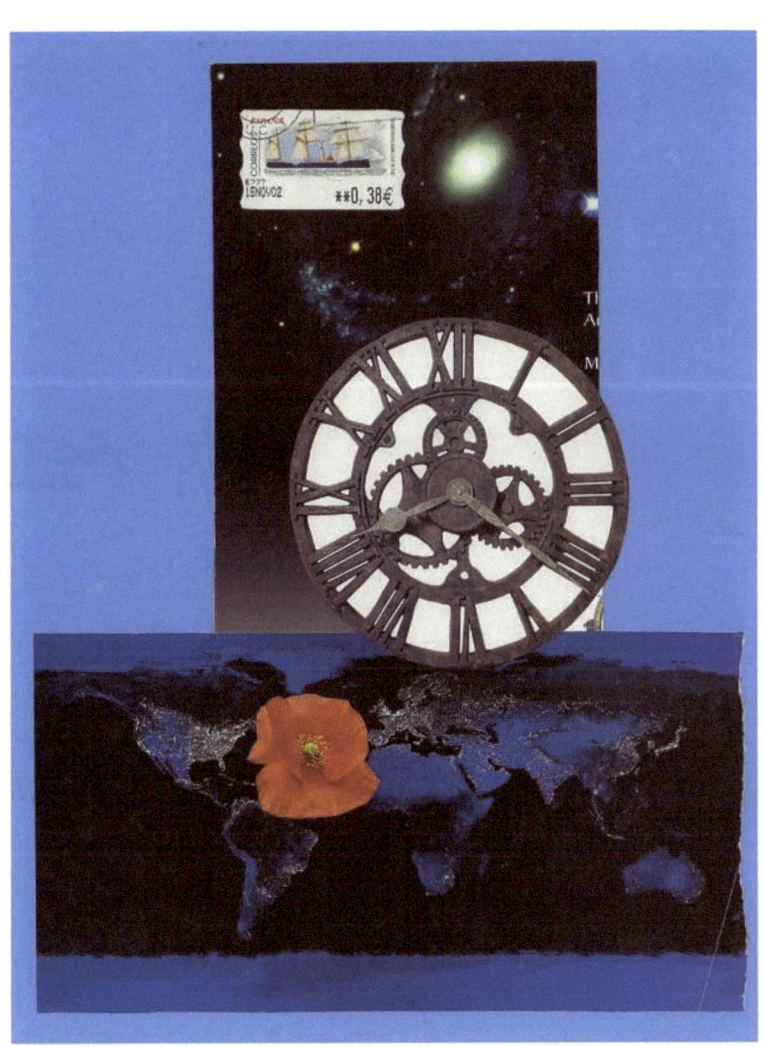

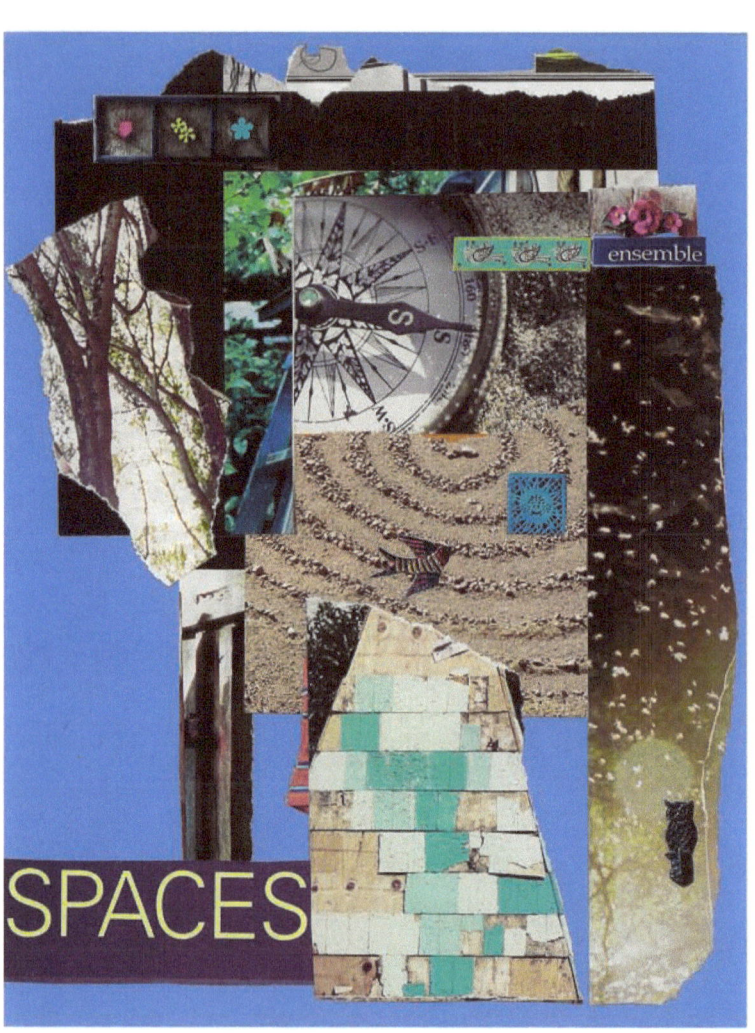

observing the sea

slip into disappearance

where the sky is a waterfall
& the story a net to be cut

where the architecture
is a wave or maybe a flower

*

the library of the moon
equates to disarm the world

unknown figures
walk the shore

the landscape
is a door

*

trace

the

astronomy

of

a

tree

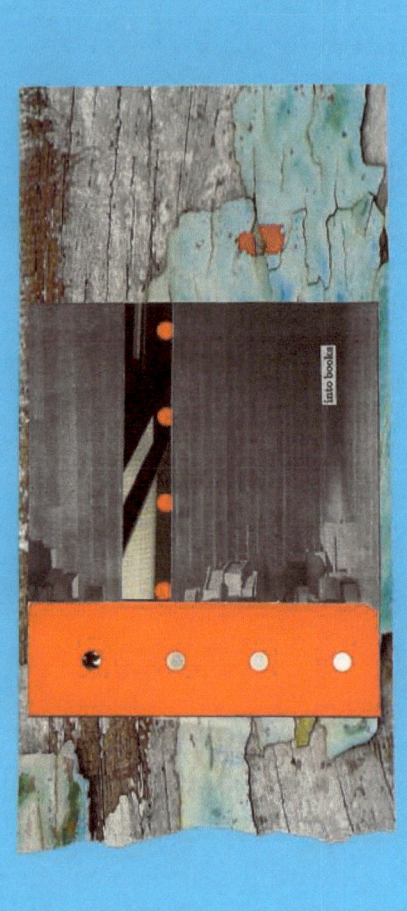

porcelain & paintings

fish flower bird.   wind wave cloud.
the years.   the walks.   the lampposts.
violets & costumes.   to read another book.
impatient the desire for illumination.

*

utopia the morning

the blue canoe
rises from the page

Berryman's *Dream Songs*
Agnes Martin's *Writings*

Frankenthaler's *Basque Beach
Mountains and Sea*

labyrinths & maps

        piecing together

birds & forests

        chameleons

across clouds

        parenthesis wood

weaving then unraveling

        the ornithologist

            the traveler

thimbles

        suns & moons

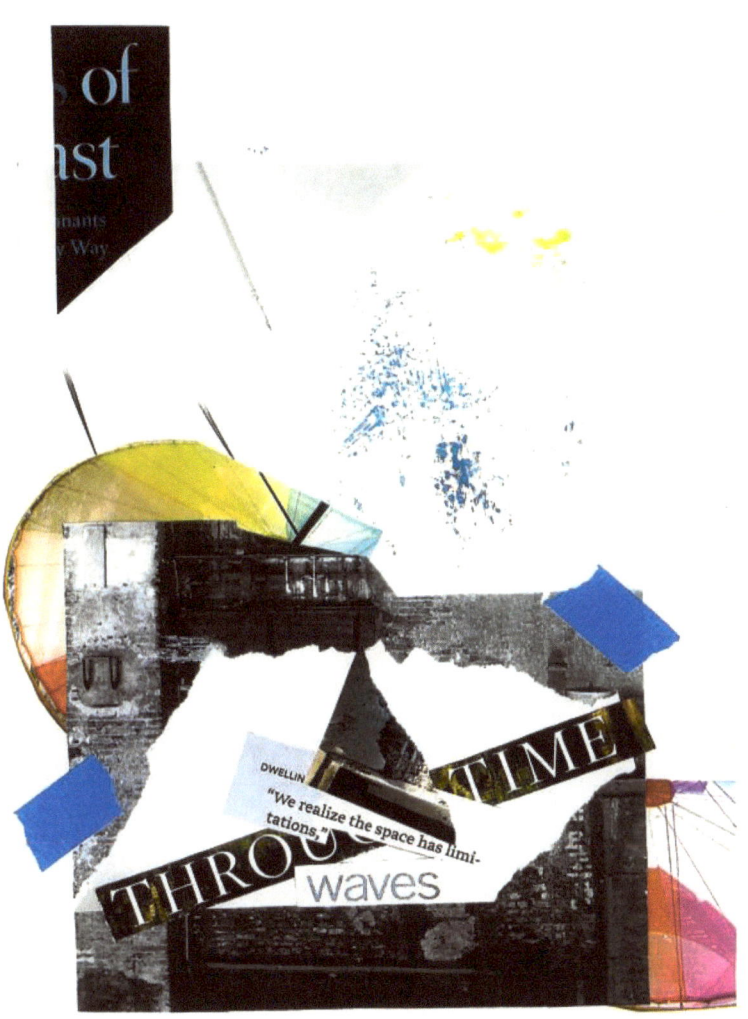

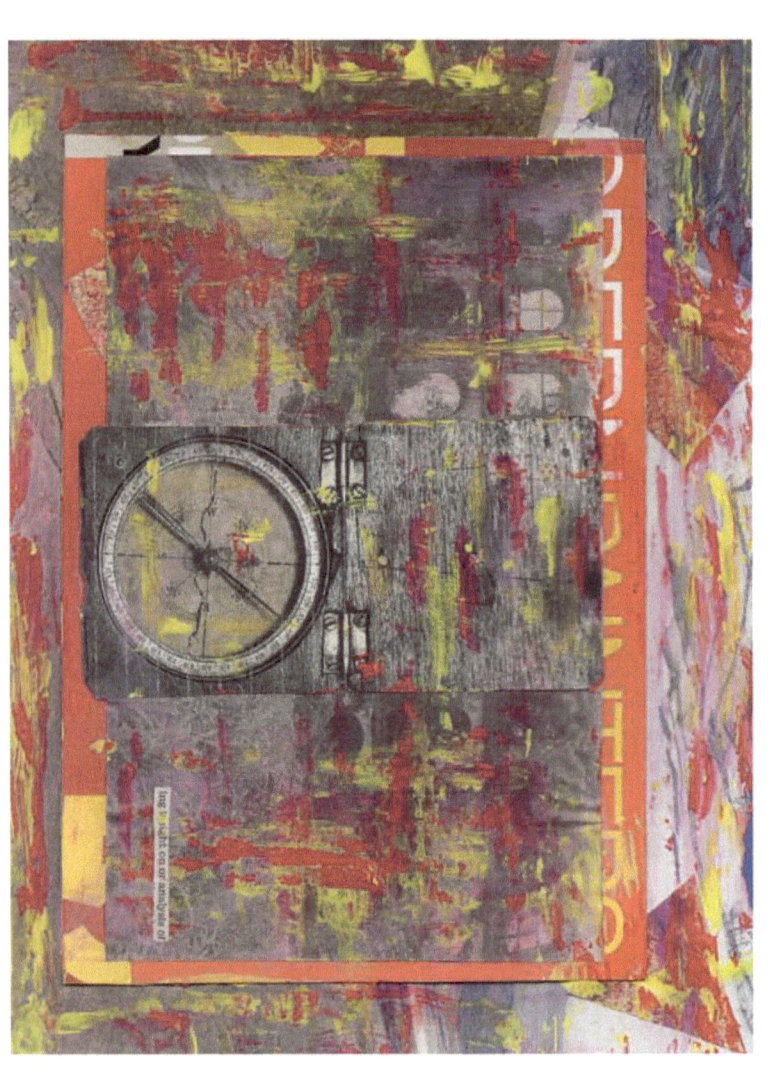

in the silence

of wind & memories   roads   hours   meadows   roots   dreams

Neruda's   *flight of the spirit*   Krasner's *Art brings about art*

*

the windows

& the tree's branches   rabbits & dogs   blue tape   watercolors

a path in Spain   undercurrents   waves   an altered book

poem paintings composed in the mind   calculate nothing

*

there is no chronological order

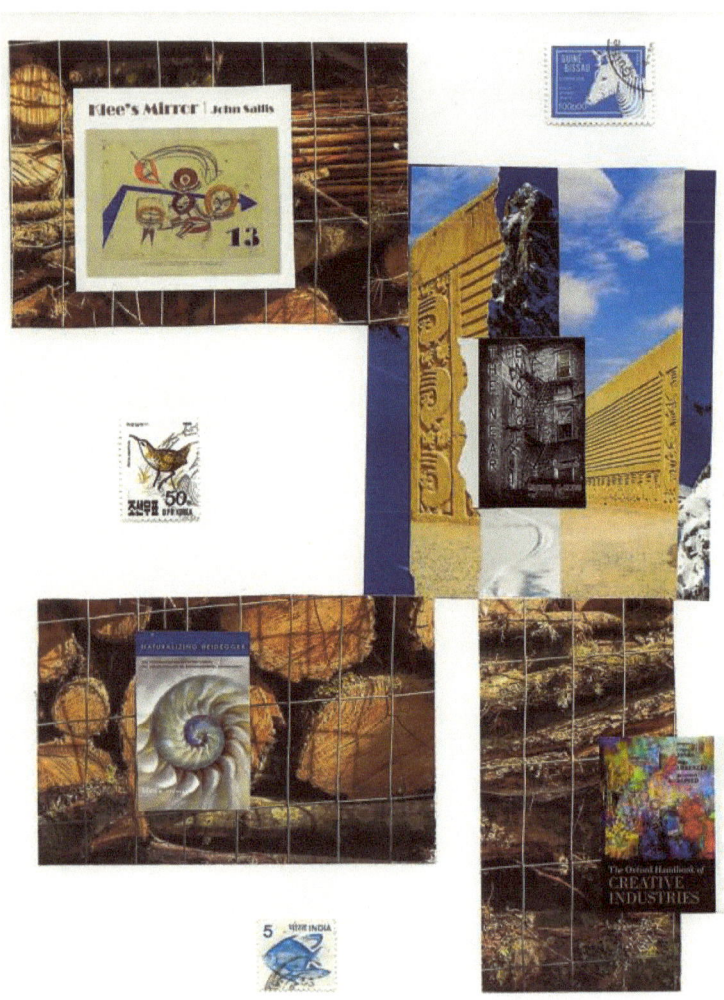

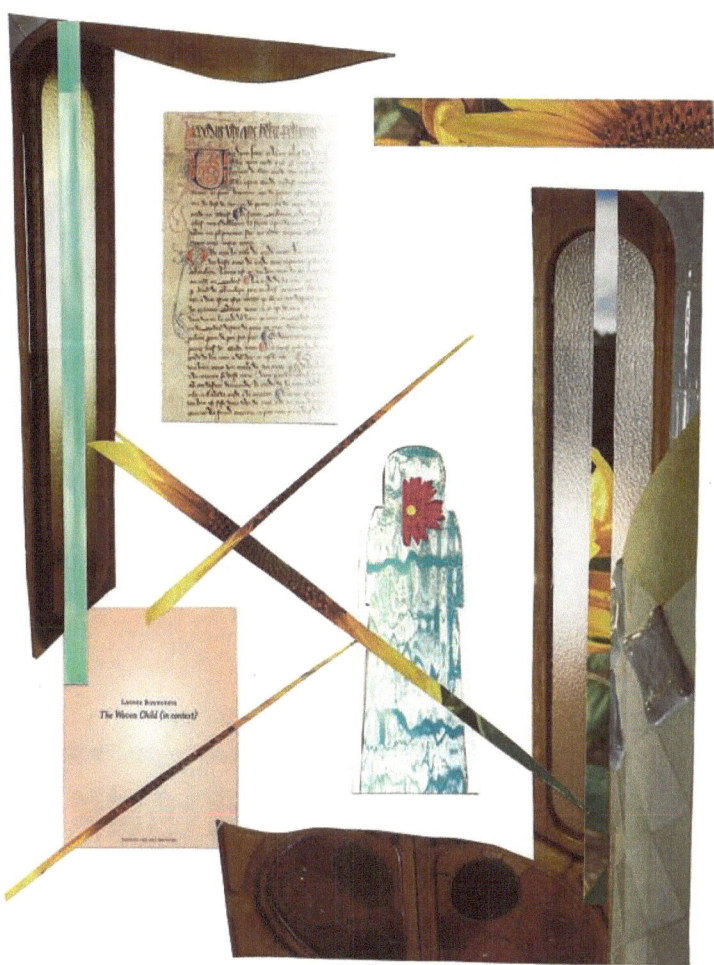

rewrite the margins

spiral crosscurrents   darkness light   simultaneous shells
caregiver trauma   contemporary lies   lines abandoned
the self a petroglyph   tradition discovered   interwoven
caves & fields   threads & circles   ratio foray sandstone
walls responsible   sun figures   handprints   hollow reeds
against stone   surface   woman/deer

*

ideology identity

discernable notes of a Mozart sonata or the reality of impossible

philosophy the stars   reference *mereology*
                [the logic of the relationship
                        of part to whole]

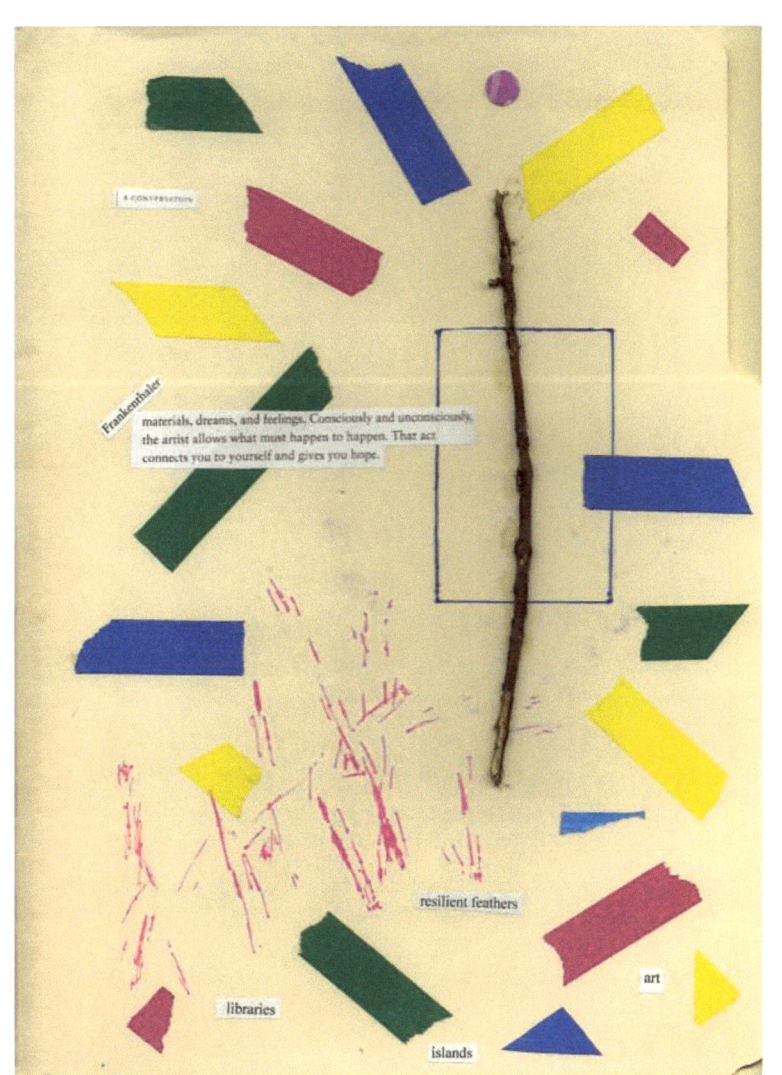

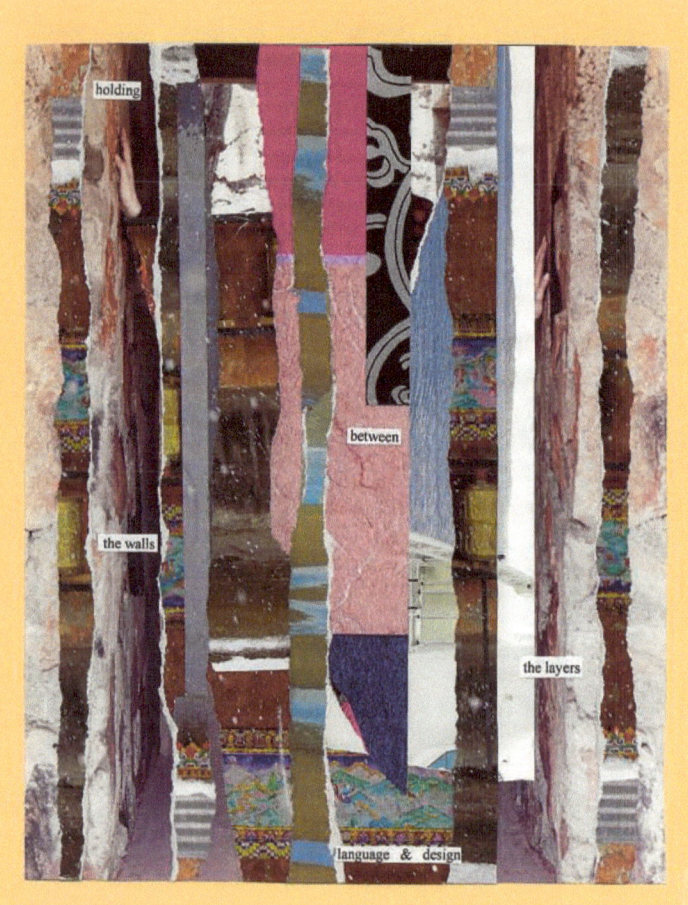

metamorphic contrary

passage verse inventing leaf inventing stone stitching
time inside/outside the wave
patterns windows hands peninsulas archetypal river
condition existence
I gather twigs or maybe abandoned ideas

*

possible/impossible

poetry structures the ascent partakes of
the syllable from mystic to stoic to saint
perhaps a soliloquy perhaps a rebellion
the sky as geography the soil as memory

a white owl feather drifts by

Kandinsky. music.   architecture. Varo.
sand. sea.   sea stars. blue green threads. red.
railroad tracks. compasses. ancient maps.
through clouds.   on a stairway.   walking through.

*

reflections

open doors

into rivers

griffins & storms & stars

unmoored

traveling

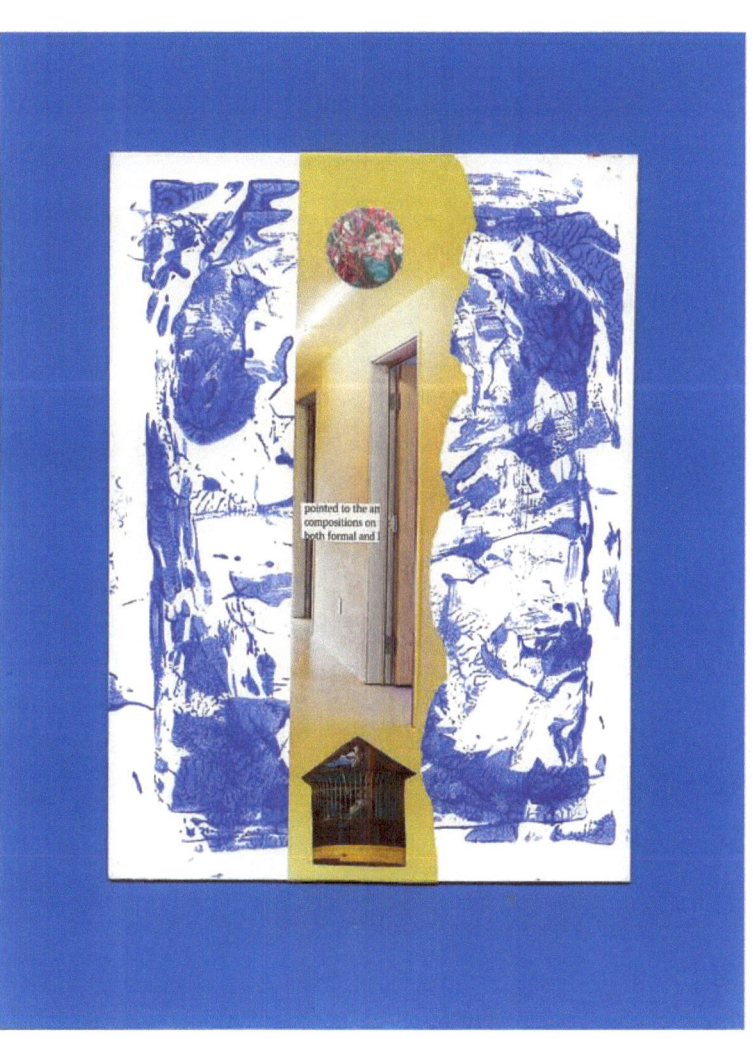

islands

imagination/reality. mind/world. perception/image.
incorporated. diminished.
the blues & the avant-garde. sloped.
circle fragments. world/mind.

*

unstitch the risk

unstructure the language

the wilderness is a state of mind

nothing is inconsequential

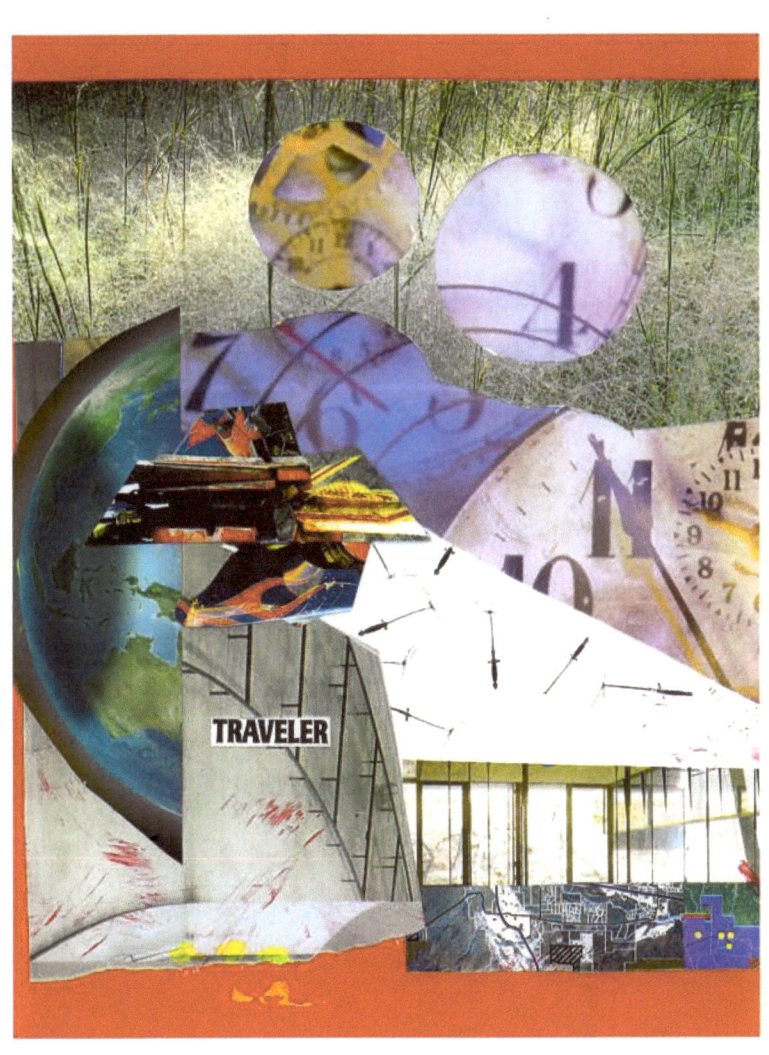

conversations

inner mobility
Jack London

nonchronological pencil drawing poems
dreams in blue reasons rectangles a canvas
a painting images objects ideas—shells
pinecones stones—transformation stages
uncharted black ink

*

unbound

a handmade book with red thread

voyaging   assembled   enveloped

the candle   smashed porcelain

Frankenthaler   Yeats   Hoffman

transcend   transparent   unveiled

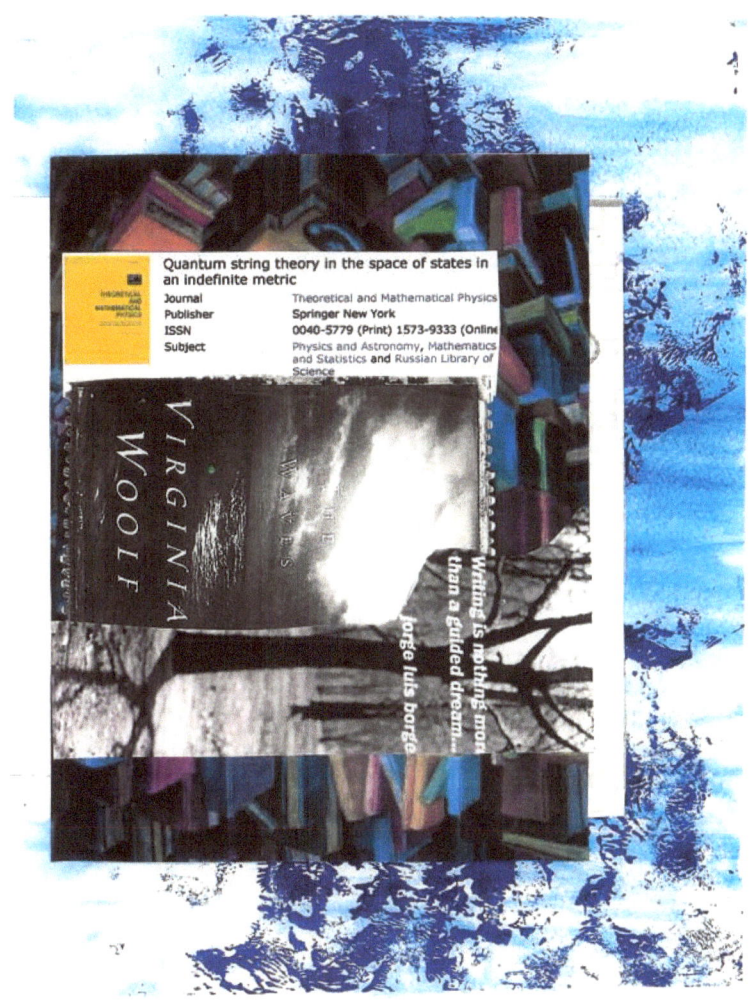

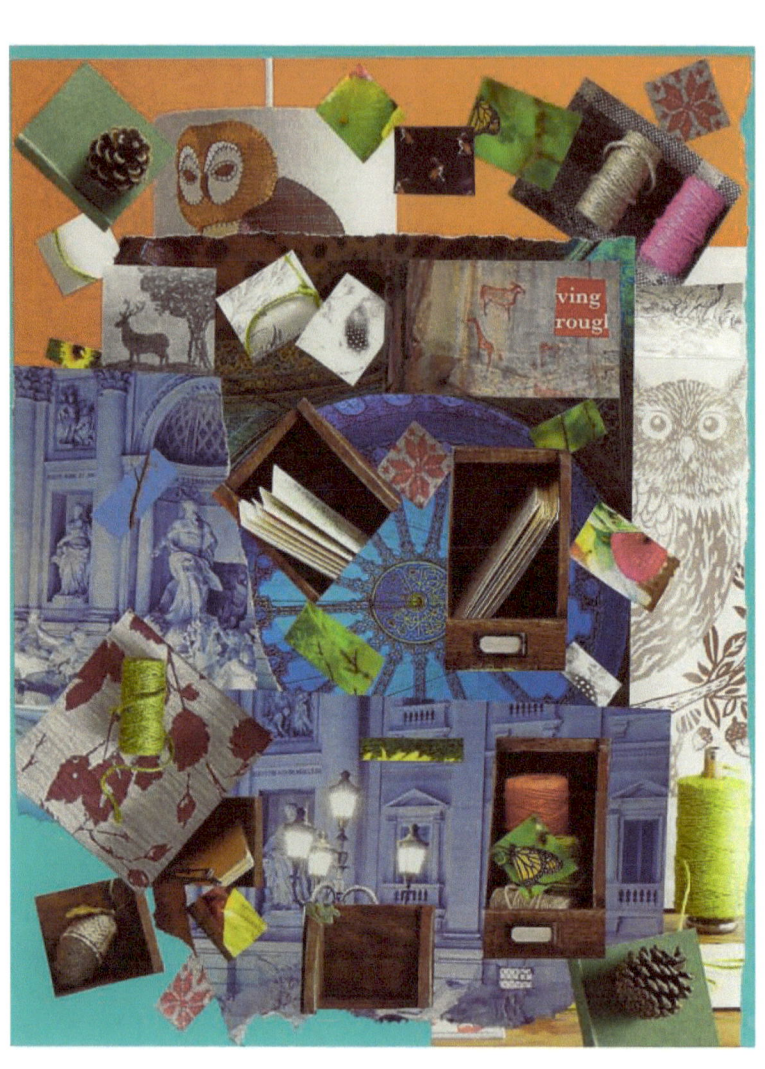

against the edge

my life

as waves

overthrown

garments

of chance

of stitchery

the maps many

the bridge

once

against

the tides

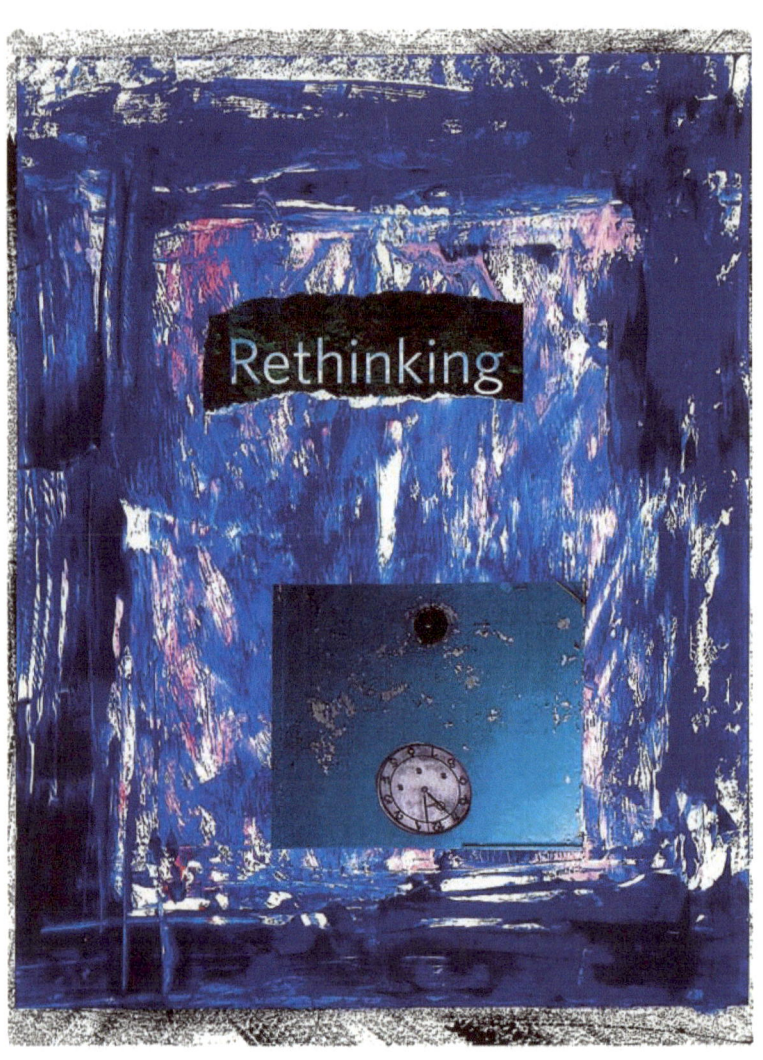

caterpillar ant hedgehog

we enter the world
through
secret passageways

open boxes
climb walls

we wander
outside
the ordinary
camouflaged
in
language
or
maybe
drawings

keys
hang
from
trees

we
subvert
haiku
into
psychology
or
maybe
rhythm
random

at a distance

spaces   heads   gardens
sky   music   years
inventions

through a means   measure of
ever moving

windmills   silence   doors
journeys   undetermined
traces

sustained   visions   light
integrated by oaks & rain

*

en los sueños

after Remedios Varo

we create trees from invisible poems
& journeys through forests & clouds
the wings — flowers   dragons   birds   stars

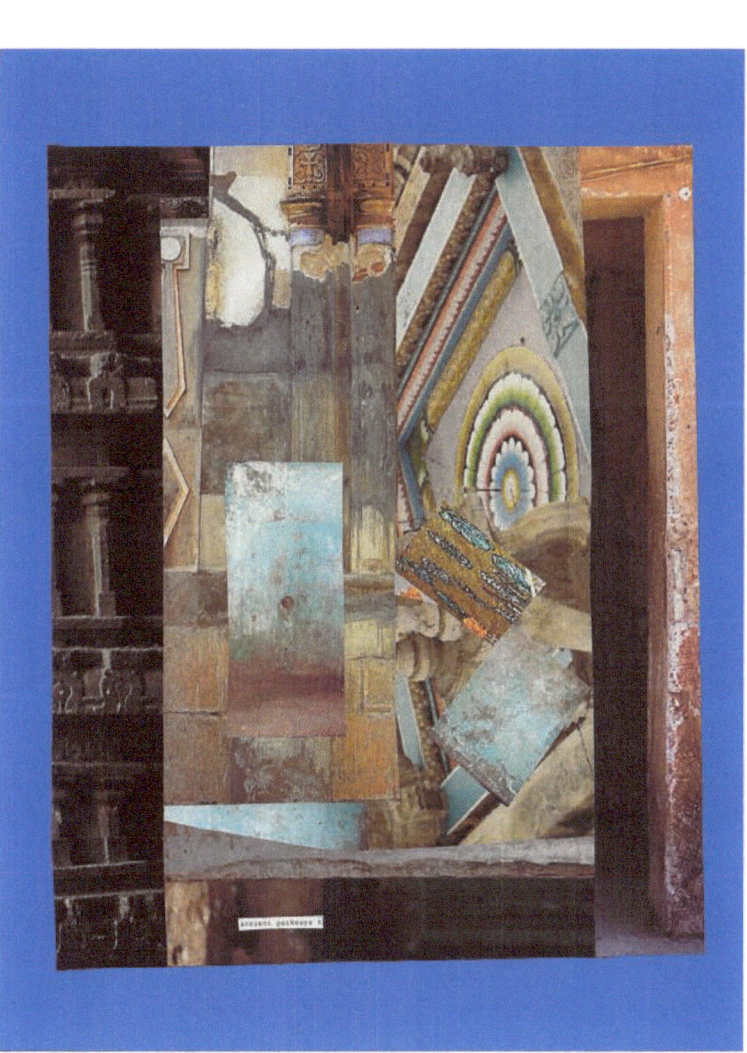

"In her
drawin[g]"

Dr. ... recently discovered ... additional evidence points to the fact that Akhenaten, with her own interwoven interpretation ... it is said that Akhenaten, with her delicacies, and beside her, was no more monogamous than

... jars of w... showing Akhenaten and ... Amarna art. The ... is the sheer ... But what str... father of all liv... his sole god as ... the Aten" in w... from Akhenate[n] ... inscriptions are ... owner of the ... invariably depict... touch the royal ... rays endi[ng] ... shown ... no god a... Egyptian histor... somewhat ignomin... was ... one who, a... naten ... the circle of ... But h... governm[en]t religious ... which was stiff and ... the conventional ... flowers and plant ... depicting ... escape ... dynasty ... like ... building ... even ... mud-br... disappeared ... The c... itself has largely ... cuneiform writing in which ... Amarna is likely to forget it. ... one who has visited Tell el-... from ... clay tablets in the Babylonian ... letters.

whom, Ankhespaaten (later re-named Ankhesenamun), became the wife of Tutankhamun. No ... neglected his foreign dominions, ... evidence for this is provided ... Beketaten, to whom she is handing a tasty morsel of food ... sits her own little daughter, absorbed in his new religion,

sleeping under/with the moon

the artist's life is a fragile life

a speck of yellow. a line of blue.

windstorms. waves.

bridges made of glass.

reading Unamuno. reading Kierkegaard.

mountain wilderness.

wild parrots. canyon birds.

*

impossible misfits   5:05

the awareness isolated avoids analysis to emphasize the narrative
we live in shoeboxes or maybe shoes conversations like portraits
of the abstract we confirm bittersweet acknowledge truth beyond control to justify nothing

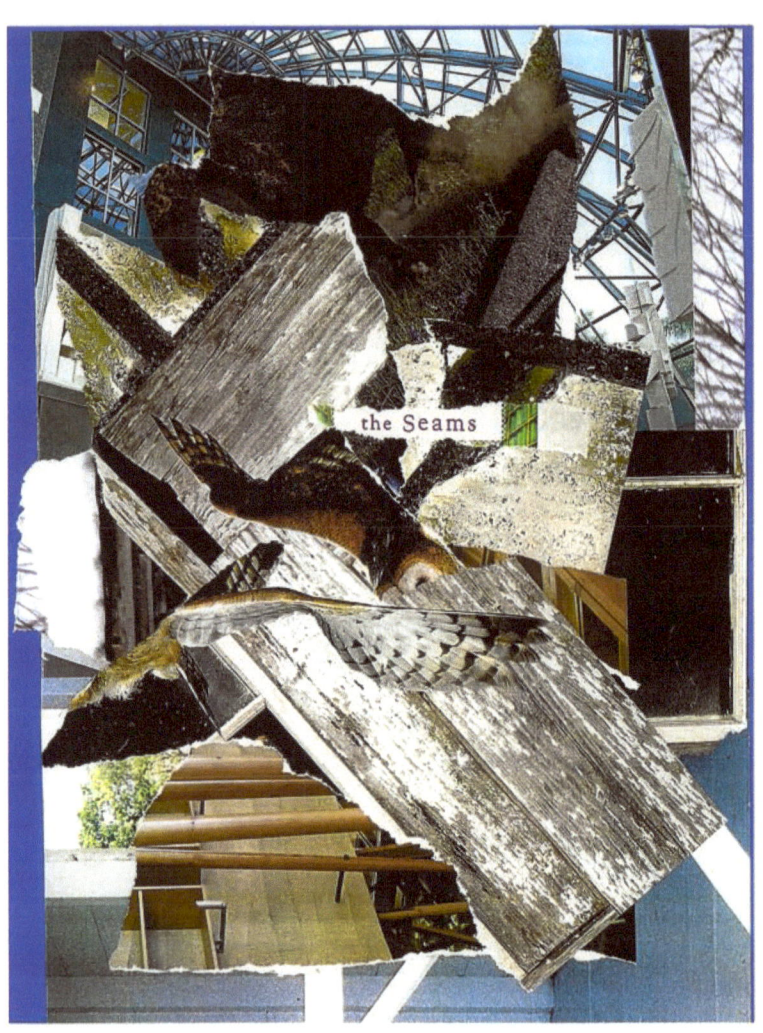

through the glass field

layer the colors   the confessions   sunflowers   wisteria

the Madonna   the mountains   cobalt   cerulean

anonymous angels & demons

*

storyboard the story

      the life in search the life in contemplation the life in flight syllable the moment

earth sky water the philosopher the fisherman the seamstress

nomads of the mind   tides & rhythms & threads

*

disentangle

conscious/unconscious

Spain. Japan.

windmills. trees in snow.

in search of the luminous.

open the window. sleep.

walk the earth.

there are dreams in paintings.

the world is a globe with wings

Vida

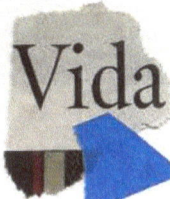

THE CONTEMPORARY

"Ahora las cosas del Arte nacen de abajo como las flores."
Roberto Matta

forward

through the surreal
time spaces
circles within the abstract

*

white rabbits & muses

Leonora Carrington   Remedios Varo

bees in the garden   owls in the oaks

flowers   &   angels   &   books

a sparrow   a lion   a dragonfly

& in the benediction   a language of the invisible

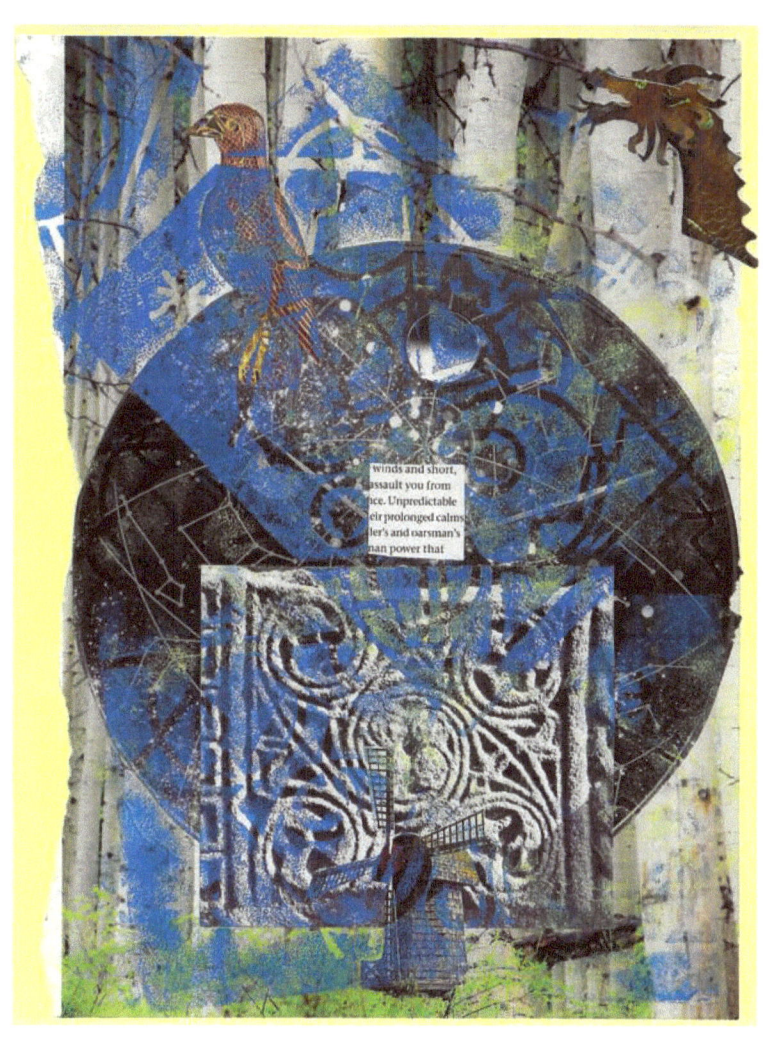

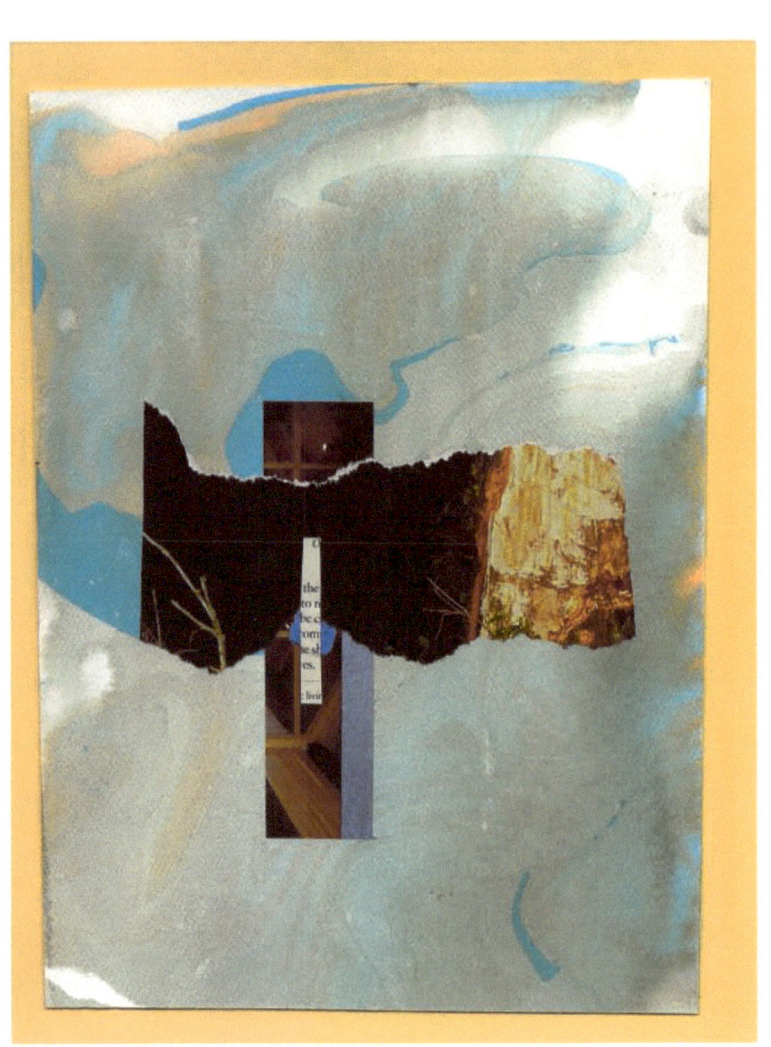

between Kandinsky & time

*Who needs to know the time? It's always either too late,
or too early.*
from Chekov's *Journey*

the direction of time.
the time of direction.
omniscience.   free will.
analytical drawings.

painting with white lines

*

*Time is nothing but the form of the inner sense, that is,
of the intuition of ourselves and of our inner state…
because this inner intuition yields no shape, we endeavor
to make up for this want by analogies.*
from Kant's *Critique of Pure Reason*

color study—5 squares with concentric rings

*

poems art waves wings wires
the word *echo* appears
random probability cause & effect
clocks & molecules

glass painting with sun

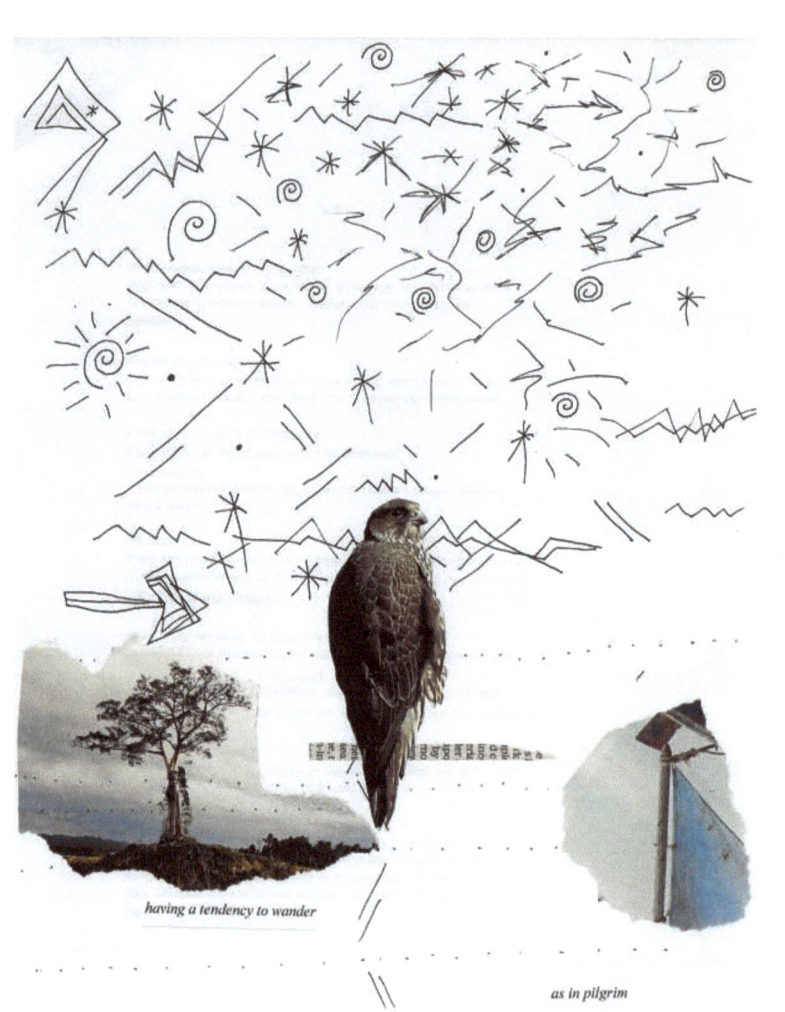

having a tendency to wander

as in pilgrim

restless

manifests the sword

where
the idea

equals
vision

&

the sanctuary
is a sun

discovered
within

unintimidated
by convention

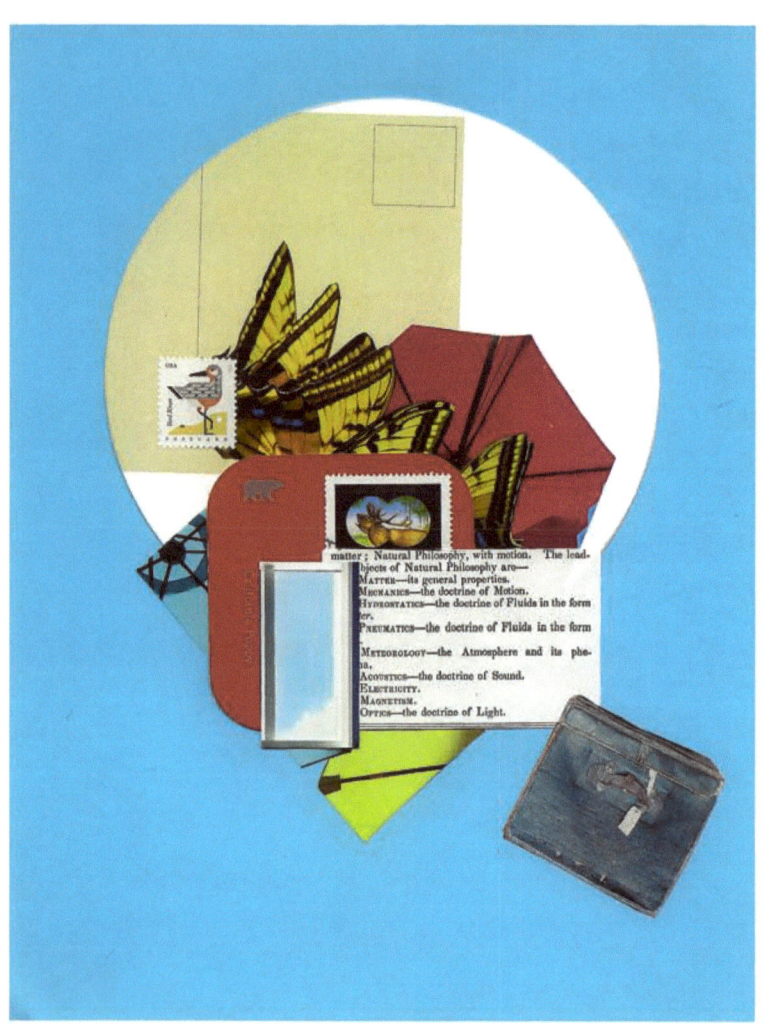

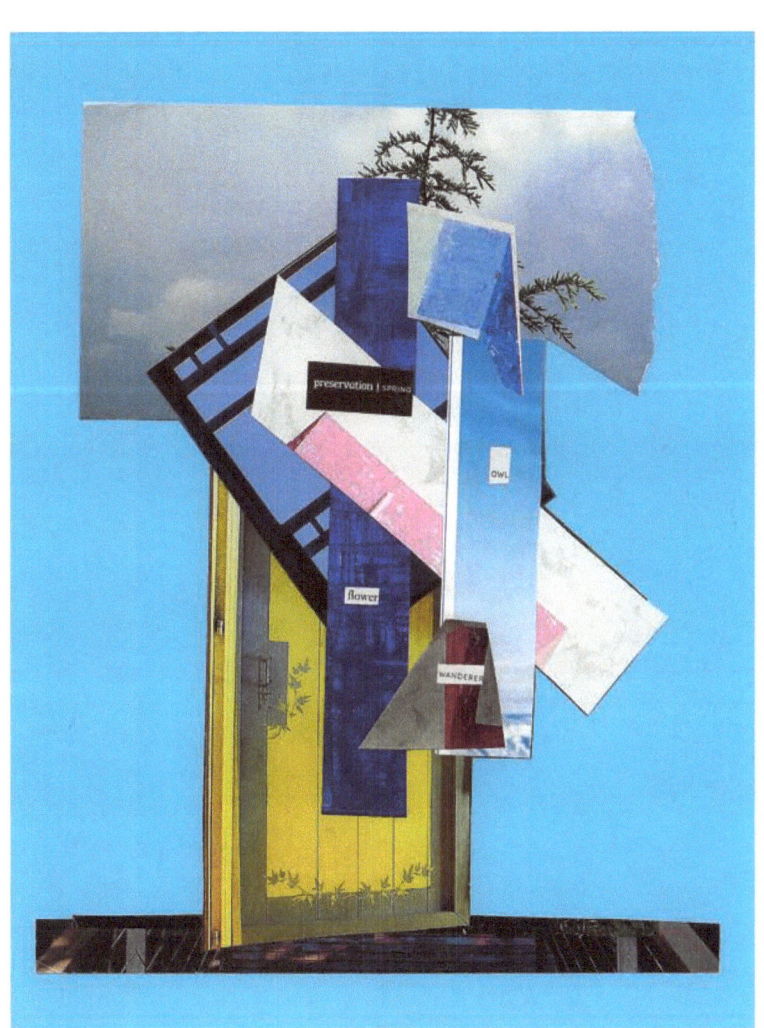

traveler

a portal

of forms

opens

daydreams

survival

daydreams

ascend

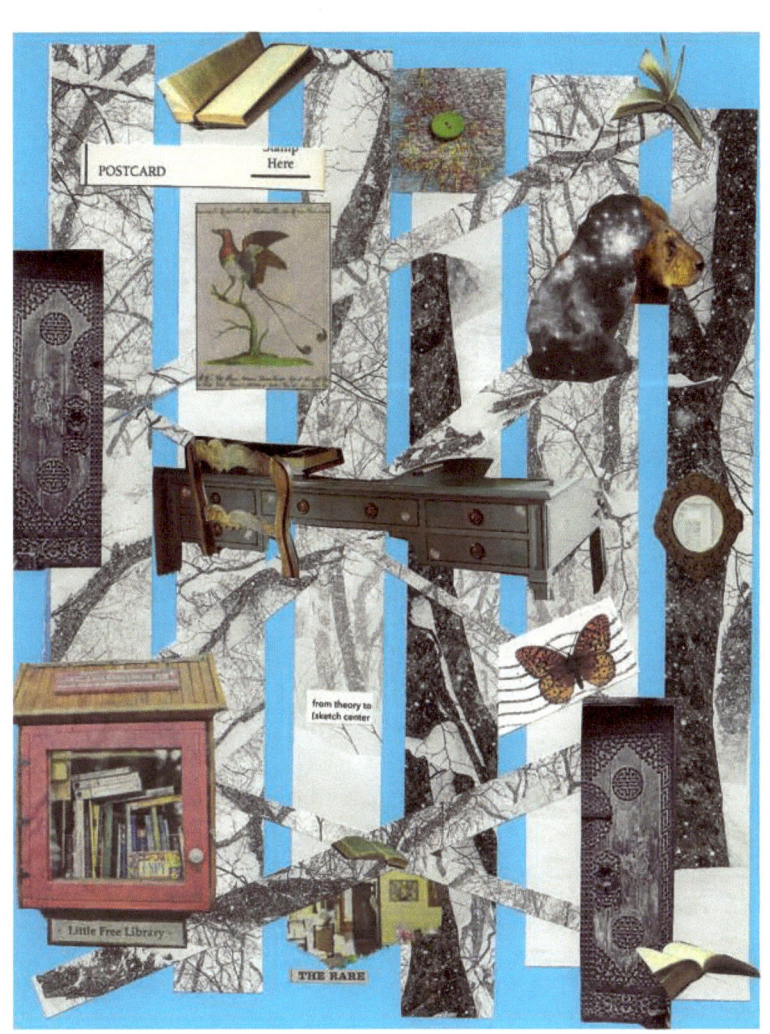

crosswinds

pioneers
self-reliance

abstract
country

*

the stream
after rain

an acorn
a stone

*

art comes from art
Agnes Martin

intervals
handmade

*

carved
driftwood

canyon
branch

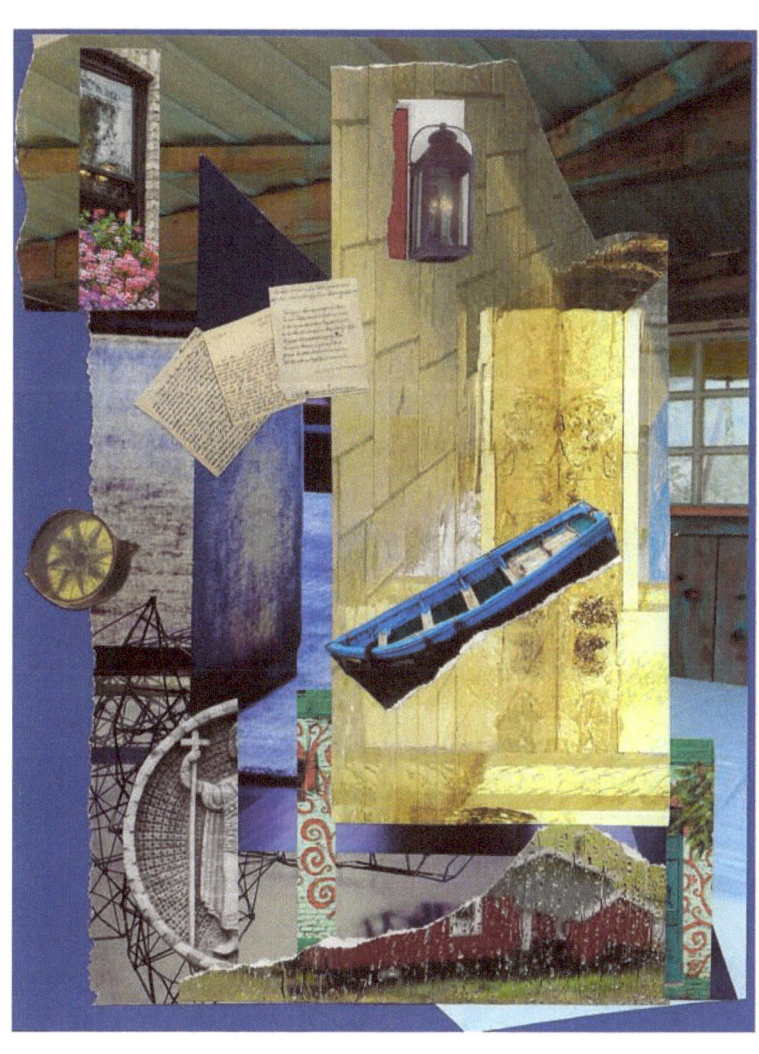

www.ingramcontent.com/pod-product-compliance
Lightning Source LLC
Chambersburg PA
CBHW040330220526
45473CB00009B/2630